PV9-14-120-253

SESSION PLANS

The Instructional Design Library

Volume 16

SESSION PLANS

Robert G. Godfrey
Allstate Insurance Company
Northbrook, Illinois

Danny G. Langdon
Series Editor

Educational Technology Publications
Englewood Cliffs, New Jersey 07632

Library of Congress Cataloging in Publication Data

Godfrey, Robert G
    Session plans.

    (The Instructional design library; v. no. 16)
    Bibliography: p.
    1. Group work in education. 2. Teaching—
Aids and devices. I. Title. II. Series.
LB1032.G6   371.3   77-25427
ISBN 0-87778-120-6

Printed in the United States of America.

Library of Congress Catalog Card Number:
77-25427.

International Standard Book Number:
0-87778-120-6.

First Printing: February, 1978.

FOREWORD

One has to be impressed with the simplicity of the Session Plan instructional design. Indeed, it is so simple that some instructional technologists might think that it could not possibly work in real instructional settings. There is no rule, however, which states that an instructional design has to be complex in order to be effective. In fact, it is often the case that we need instructional designs which clearly and simply communicate between teachers and their students.

The Session Plan design assists learners as well as teachers to organize their activities purposefully. While the author writes primarily for trainers in training situations, such as in corporations or the military services, teachers in all situations can benefit from the use of Session Plans.

Danny G. Langdon
Series Editor

PREFACE

This book is based in large measure on the professional experience I have gained as a member of Allstate's Home Office Training Division. I am indebted to the Training Director and to my associates, without whom the writing of this book would have been impossible.

R.G.G.

CONTENTS

ABSTRACT

SESSION PLANS

A Session Plan is an important item in any teaching or training situation because it logically directs a teacher or trainer through a given course of instruction that produces desired learning outcomes. Without a Session Plan, organization and sequence are lacking, and learning outcomes are in doubt.

Session Plans are applicable only to group instruction, although the size of the "group" can be as small as two (one instructor and one learner). However, a Session Plan has no limitations for use with different grade levels.

A Session Plan can be prepared on virtually any subject, and usually appears in one of three different formats: scripted (complete sentences), non-scripted (sentence fragments), and combination scripted and non-scripted. In addition, a Session Plan is logically organized. It has a beginning, a middle, and an end. It proceeds, in a smooth fashion, from the general to the specific. It is comprised of four main sections: introduction, procedure, practice, and wrap-up.

In order to achieve learning, instruction requires planning, perhaps even more planning today than ever before. And the key to planning effective instructional strategy is preparing a Session Plan. With its four component parts, writing a Session Plan forces an instructor to mentally walk through a class lesson before he or she actually administers it. Then, during the class, the Session Plan serves as a valuable guidance device for keeping the teacher pointed in the right direction, not without flexibility, but with reason. Finally, when the class is over, the Session Plan functions as a valuable historical record that can easily be referenced in planning future classes.

Classroom and corporate instructors at all levels will find Session Plans one of the most beneficial teaching aids available.

SESSION PLANS

I.

USE

Dan Olson confidently approached the lectern to kick off the second in a series of four "Train the Trainer" sessions. In attendance were nine newly-appointed trainers from the Enterprise Corporation's Service Department. All of the attendees had roughly three to five years of supervisory experience, and they had all conducted informal training sessions from time to time, but none had ever served as a full-time, professional trainer.

As it turned out, Dan got the session rolling smoothly, and the trainees participated in several exercises designed to simulate "real-world" training conditions. In fact, all the participants in the session agreed that it was one of the most beneficial seminars they had ever experienced.

Why? What were the ingredients of this particular session that made it stand out in the minds of the trainees who attended it?

Was it the videotape gear? Definitely impressive, useful, even humorous at times, when some of the "out takes" were replayed. Of course, individual, "live" critiques of the trainees' presentations would have been almost as effective.

What about the other audio-visual aids, such as slides and flip chart sheets? These techniques, too, were used appropriately and effectively. If they hadn't been incorporated in the seminar, it might have suffered, but probably only a little.

The trainers were excellent. They were knowledgeable and enthusiastic, and really did a fine job tying the four days of the seminar together.

However, it is not inconceivable that the seminar could have been set up as a self-study course. Also, the number of trainers could have been reduced from three to two or even to one, thus de-emphasizing their impact and influence on the session.

Why a Session Plan Is Important

When you think about it, there is only one component of the Enterprise Corporation's Train the Trainer session that was indispensable: the Session Plan. Without it, nothing would have happened. You need a Session Plan to put the parts of your training program together into a functional whole. *The Session Plan is the most important item in any training program.* Let's see how a Session Plan was used in the Train the Trainer seminar, and then we can establish the importance of this valuable training tool.

From Dan Olson's first word in his welcoming remarks to his final "Good-bye, thanks for coming," every phase, nearly every spoken line, was planned in advance and recorded in the Session Plan for Train the Trainer. Dan's purpose in preparing this plan was to establish a guide, or road map, for himself and for his trainers to follow from their "departure" on the first day until their "arrival" on the last day. Fortunately, none of the trainers missed any of the scheduled classes. But even if they had, and a different trainer had had to step in in an emergency, he or she would have felt comfortable simply by following the Session Plan.

Limitations of Session Plans

Session Plans are limited only to the extent that they are superfluous with self-study courses. As a matter of fact, self-study courses could actually be considered Session Plans themselves because they both guide the learner over a path of instruction leading from the departure (entry level) to the arrival (accomplishment of objectives). You don't need a Session Plan in order to take a self-study course. All you need to do is follow the course directions.

Session Plan Applications

Session Plans are applicable to group instruction. The size of the group could vary between one trainer and one trainee, or "one-on-one," to multiple trainers and trainees. No matter how it is used, a Session Plan should be regarded as primarily an administrative vehicle for helping a trainer provide instruction to one or more trainees. A Session Plan is not an independent tool; it must be supplemented by a qualified trainer and/or other support devices, such as slides or videotape. Instead of doing all the work itself, the Session Plan helps or guides the training administrator along the simplest, most effective path toward accomplishing the desired objectives. Together, and working in concert, the trainer and the Session Plan can do the job. Individually, regardless of how skilled or how detailed, each is bound to run into a certain number of roadblocks, delays, and detours.

Fortunately, a Session Plan has no limitations for use with different grade levels. A kindergarten teacher, for example, can use a Session Plan as effectively as a college professor or an industrial trainer. The complexity of their Session Plans varies significantly, but everybody who teaches or trains needs what only a Session Plan can provide: organization, application, and direction.

A Session Plan can be prepared on virtually any subject, and it can approach each topic in three different ways: scripted, non-scripted, and combination. All of these approaches are presented, analyzed, and illustrated in the

Operational Description and Design Format sections of this book.

The single criterion that determines whether or not a Session Plan should be prepared is not the nature of the subject, but rather the method in which the subject is to be presented. If a subject will be presented in a self-study format, for example, a Session Plan won't be very useful. The self-study course will provide all of the directional guidance required by the learner. If the subject is to be presented in a formal classroom environment by a qualified stand-up trainer, however, then either a scripted, non-scripted, or combination Session Plan is in order.

Session Plans can be prepared on subjects ranging from shoe-tying to statistical coding. The subject matter of the training session is not a criterion for deciding whether or not to use Session Plans. The training session, however, should be appropriate for the use of Session Plans. Self-study courses are really the only examples of instruction formats that can't benefit from Session Plans. In all other instruction formats, where "live" trainers are used, Session Plans can be used to effectively organize the training session.

As a general idea of what Session Plans can be applied to, following is a list of examples of teaching and training situations that are appropriate for session plans in school and in business.

School. Music, physical education, reading, art, geology, psychology, English literature, etc., as long as these subjects are taught by a live, stand-up teacher or trainer and are not self-studied.

Business. Sales training, transactional analysis, management development, etc., as long as these types of subject matter aren't self-studied, through programmed instruction, computer-assisted instruction, or some other form of self-tutoring device.

II.

OPERATIONAL DESCRIPTION

One of the best ways to see how a Session Plan works is to experience, vicariously, how a trainer uses his or her Session Plan. Let's see how Dan Olson capitalized on the Session Plan techniques in his Train the Trainer session for Enterprise Corporation. In fact, Figure 1 is the actual Session Plan Dan used for his opening remarks. Let's walk through it, step by step.

Format

The Session Plan for Dan's introduction couldn't have been simpler. The format is simple, the layout is spartan. There are only five entries, and they are in topic outline format. And yet, as we've already seen, Dan was able to pick up this Session Plan and "run with it." Why? How could such a simple organizational tool help Dan deliver a dynamic introduction?

Time

As soon as Dan looked at the Session Plan, he noticed one very critical item: the length of time the introduction was supposed to last. Dan knew, of course, long before he checked his Session Plan, how long he could spend on the introduction. His prior knowledge had told him he had a lot to do in just twenty minutes. But the session plan reminded him, right up front: twenty minutes to cover five areas. In

Figure 1

Sample Session Plan

4/28/77

INTRODUCTION
8:40 - 9:00

√1. Write down perceptions, hold, review at end of evaluation.
    A.   Job.
    B.   Week.

 2. Objectives.

 3. Job Description.

 4. Agenda—1st day only.

 5. Ground rules.
    A.   Notes & notebooks.
    B.   Sessions start on time.
    C.   Questions.

Dan's case, then, the time entry at the top of his session plan served as a valuable alarm.

Introduction

Item number one is another piece of coded input for Dan. In fact, Dan considered this point all-important in getting his Train the Trainer Workshop off to a fast, interesting pace. He wanted to be friendly, and yet he wanted to avoid the standard opening remarks clichés. He thought that by asking the trainees to note their perceptions of their roles as trainers on the first day, they'd be interested in comparing them with their understanding of their job on the last day of the seminar. And Dan's Session Plan told him to cover perceptions the very first thing on the agenda. But at the last minute, something flashed in his mind.

"It dawned on me," Dan said, "that there we were, about to get all involved in how the trainers saw their roles, and I'd forgotten to make the necessary introductions.

"I shifted gears in the middle of a sentence, and switched to an interview approach for the introductions. It worked out pretty well, but my Session Plan saved me.

"It seems strange, but 'make introductions' not being included in the Session Plan was what brought it to my attention. It was an obvious omission. And since my Session Plan was flexible, I decided on the spot to run a little past our cut-off point to accommodate the interviews and introductions."

After Dan completed the introductions, he got his opening remarks back on track by returning to point number one. In a single sentence, Dan's Session Plan reminded him to cover a large amount of information. To expand the Session Plan, the trainees were supposed to write, in their own words, exactly how they saw themselves, as of that particular minute in time, functioning as trainers. In addition, trainees were to fold up their papers and put them aside until the end of the session. If the perceptions were out of sight, the trainees wouldn't be tempted to revise them. The purpose of the exercise, of course, was to determine to what extent the trainees' original perceptions of their roles as trainers changed as a result of Train the Trainer.

The next item on the session plan is a simple, one-word entry: objectives. When Dan saw this notation, it cued him to a flip chart, which he positioned in the front of the classroom. The first flip chart sheet contained a list of objectives stated in behavioral terms that Dan was easily able to cover and develop fully. All of this important information was unlocked as a result of a one-word key on a Session Plan.

After reviewing the objectives, Dan noticed that the Session Plan called for covering the job description of the seminar participants. Without wasting any time and without fumbling, Dan presented a large poster board containing a detailed write-up of the job description, mounted it in a stand where everybody could read it clearly, and proceeded to conduct an in-depth discussion of what the new trainers were expected to accomplish.

Procedure and Practice

From reviewing the trainers' job description, Dan turned to the Train the Trainer agenda. The Session Plan, however, called for reviewing the agenda for the first day only. Momentarily, Dan couldn't remember why he should review only the first day, but that didn't make any difference. Dan was confident about the Session Plan, and even if his mind temporarily went blank, which isn't an uncommon occurrence for stand-up trainers, he could have the discussion about the agenda come about as if it had been rehearsed every day for a week.

Wrap-Up

The fifth point in Dan's Session Plan, ground rules, is really the only item on which any elaboration is supplied. Of course, a Session Plan can be set up to supply virtually a limitless amount of supportive detail, or the Session Plan can be strictly skeletal, furnishing no more than the absolute minimum of information required to get the session moving and to keep it rolling.

Dan reasoned that since the ground rules portion of his introduction would directly affect the participants on an everyday basis, he wanted to review the ground rules without missing a single point. From sub-topics A through C under item five, Dan was successfully able to elaborate on the critical details. He explained that since handout material would be provided, the participants would not have to take notes. In addition, binders would be available for storing and organizing the handouts. From his Session Plan, Dan also remembered to remind the learners that the sessions would start on time. In fact, Dan explained that the sessions would start on time even if there were stragglers. Finally, Dan's Session Plan contained a very important reminder about questions. Dan's experience had taught him that if a question policy isn't established during the embryonic stage of a training session, much confusion and wasted time can result. Therefore, using his Session Plan as a cue, Dan explained that during the Train the Trainer session, he'd like participants to hold their questions until the trainer called for them. That way, presentations would proceed to their logical conclusions without being hacked apart before they were finished. Dan suggested to the participants that as they come up with questions during the presentations, they should jot them down in order to remember them later during the question and answer period.

Summary of Components

We have completed walking through Dan Olson's Session Plan for the Train the Trainer Introduction. We have seen it from his perspective, almost as if we ourselves were the instructor. In summary, it is interesting to note that each part of Dan's Session Plan represents a part of Session Plans in general. For example, Dan's Session Plan, like most, is concerned with covering a block of information with a predetermined time frame. This time frame may or may not be flexible, but time is usually a consideration in administering the session.

In addition, Dan's Session Plan, again, like most others, is logically organized. It has a beginning, a middle, and an end. It proceeds, in a smooth fashion, from the general to the specific. It is designed to attract the trainees' interest, and then to hold, even to increase, that interest. In fact, these common denominators of all Session Plans could be labeled as follows: introduction, procedure, practice, and wrap-up.

To use Dan's Session Plan as an example, the introduction would consist of items one, two, and three; the procedure and practice would be item four; and the wrap-up would be item five. These labels and their applications will be explained and discussed in detail in the Design Format section of this book.

Impact of Session Plans on Trainers and Trainees

Now let's see how the trainees reacted to Dan's Session Plan. Although the Session Plan is primarily a trainer-oriented vehicle, as mentioned earlier, it is, of course, imperative that the Session Plan produce results; that the *learners* benefit from it.

For openers, the format of the Session Plan makes little, if any, difference to the learner; he or she never actually sees it. Whether the Session Plan is carefully detailed on a four-color,

35mm slide, or whether it's scrawled on the back of an envelope, the trainee gets the same message. The trainee is primarily concerned with the content and organization of the training session, as spelled out in the Session Plan, and with the learning that results, not with the outward appearance of the instructor's Session Plan.

Some instructors, for the sake of convenience, do like to prepare slides or overhead transparencies of their Session Plans to show the learners. Used this way, Session Plans can serve as combination Session Plans and agendas. Since Session Plans so often contain guidance devices for the instructor, however, they can confuse the trainees, who would be viewing the Session Plan only from the standpoint of a topical outline of the course content.

As mentioned earlier, Dan benefited significantly by noting the time factor written on the Session Plan for his introduction to Train the Trainer. This information enabled him to formulate his plan for the entire introduction. With this information, he could tailor the content of the introduction so that it would provide the required emphasis on the various points covered in the introduction, and so that the introduction would conclude as scheduled, without infringing on the sessions to follow.

The trainees, however, had absolutely no interest in the timing of the introduction. They were concerned, again, primarily with content.

They were interested in getting the Train the Trainer session off to a positive start, and in learning the skills and knowledge that composed the course. In fact, particularly during the introduction, time was probably the last thing on their minds.

Here, then, is an interesting comparison between the impact of the length of a training session, as written in the Session Plan, on the trainer and on the trainee. The time notation may significantly affect the trainer's behavior, but has only remote impact on the trainee.

On the other hand, every trainee in Dan's session was definitely interested in the introductions. All Session Plans, regardless of format, include an introductory segment. This can consist, literally, of introducing the instructor to the trainees and of introducing the trainees to each other. The introductory phase may also involve introducing the subject matter of the training session to the trainees. In either case, the importance of introductions should not be underestimated.

The introduction in Dan's Session Plan includes items one, two, and three. Without this introduction, Dan would have enough material to make a presentation, but it would probably be ineffective; the trainees wouldn't be able to see the remainder of the session in the proper perspective. In Figure 2, then, on the impact scale, the introduction phase of a Session Plan affects trainees more significantly than trainers. Whereas the trainees do not care about the format of a Session Plan and how long the session is supposed to last, they are definitely interested in the introductory phase of the session.

Of even greater importance to the trainees is what they experience following the introduction in a typical session: the so-called procedure. This is the nitty-gritty of the Session Plan, the bones on which all the meat is placed. In Dan's introductory session for Train the Trainer, for example, the procedure is item four. This is the point where the instructor reviews the first day's agenda to provide trainees with an overview of their immediate activities. The agenda, particularly the first day's events, is the point in the session where the objective should be accomplished; all of the other items to be covered in this session are incidental. Without including the first day's agenda as the main ingredient of Dan's Session Plan, however, the trainees might as well bypass the session

Figure 2

*Impact of Components
of Session Plan*

ASPECT:	IMPACT OF A SESSION PLAN ON:	
	TRAINER	TRAINEE
1. Format	Low-Medium	Low
2. Time Frame	High	Low
3. Introduction*	Low	High
4. Procedure*	High	High
5. Practice*	Medium	High
6. Wrap-Up*	Medium	Low-Medium

*Essential Component.

entirely and go directly to the first presentation. It is interesting to note that the procedure explained in a Session Plan
is also of paramount importance to trainers. A Session Plan
typically will illustrate that the seeds for accomplishing the
objectives of a training presentation are usually planted by
the instructor during the procedure.

Looking again at Figure 2, the procedure segment of a
Session Plan falls under the heading of high impact for both
trainer and trainee.

If the seeds are planted in the procedure, they are reaped
in the practice. This segment of a Session Plan is also of considerable importance to both trainers and trainees. In the
practice phase, trainees have an opportunity to try out their
newly-learned knowledge and skills and to obtain feedback
and reinforcement. The trainer, of course, needs to challenge
the learners at this point in a session, but the challenge is
greater for them because it is a new experience; trainers may
have already issued the challenge in previous sessions. Therefore, as illustrated in Figure 2, the impact of the practice phase
of a Session Plan is greater on trainees than on trainers.

Finally, the wrap-up, from the trainees' viewpoint, is help-
ful in putting it all together, so a summary of some kind is
usually noted in most Session Plans. For trainers, making an
impact this late in a training session is virtually impossible.
If the trainees haven't caught on after the introduction,
procedure, and practice phases, chances are they aren't going
to see the light at the very end. Trainees who have successfully completed the training, however, will usually benefit
from seeing everything in perspective. If nothing else, a note
at the conclusion of a Session Plan indicating wrap-up is a
good opportunity to stop for questions and answers.

By referencing Figure 2 once again, it is possible to
observe certain trends and to arrive at several conclusions.
First, a Session Plan is important to both trainers and

trainees. Second, instructors and learners disagree about which parts of a Session Plan are most important. Trainers regard a Session Plan's reference to time frames and to procedure as being most important. Trainees see the introduction, procedure, and practice segments of a Session Plan as being most important to them. In fact, trainees agree on only one generalization about Sessions Plans: The procedure section is more important than any other. There is some agreement that the format and wrap-up aspects of Session Plans are relatively unimportant.

III.

DESIGN FORMAT

As presented and discussed in the preceding Operational Description section, a Session Plan contains four *essential* parts: Introduction, Procedure, Practice, and Wrap-Up. Dan's Session Plan for his introduction to Enterprise Corporation's Train the Trainer program contains all four of these important elements. Dan's Session Plan is also noteworthy because it is non-scripted. Session Plans can also be scripted or combination non-scripted and scripted. Before reviewing the four essential parts of a Session Plan, let's study the differences between non-scripted and scripted session plans. To simplify matters, we'll concentrate on these two types of session plans now. But we'll pick up combination Session Plans later in this Design Format section.

Non-scripted Session Plans, like Dan's, are usually written in fragments; single words, notes, short phrases, incomplete sentences. This is why, in fact, they are referred to as non-scripted. Scripted Session Plans consist of complete thoughts, sentences, descriptions, and details.

To compare the two types of Session Plans, see Figures 3 and 4. Figure 3 is an example of an excerpt from a non-scripted Session Plan, like Dan's. Figure 4 is excerpted from a scripted Session Plan. Consider these two examples only in light of the format differences presented so far. Now let's turn our attention to more subtle, yet equally

Figure 3

Excerpt from a Non-Scripted Session Plan

Four essential parts of a Session Plan:

1. Introduction

2. Procedure

3. Practice

4. Wrap-Up

Figure 4

Excerpt from a Scripted Session Plan

A Session Plan contains four essential parts. They are the introduction, procedure, practice, and wrap-up.

1. The introduction sets up the entire session.

2. The procedure explains how the job is done.

3. In the practice part of a Session Plan, trainees have a chance to get their hands on the job; to learn by experiencing the real thing or a simulation.

4. The wrap-up reinforces the introduction, procedure, and practice by reviewing them.

important differences between non-scripted and scripted Session Plans.

Non-Scripted Session Plans

Although the most obvious aspect of a non-scripted Session Plan is that it is not written in complete sentences, this type of session plan contains many other distinguishing characteristics. For example, the non-scripted Session Plan attempts to provide direction to a veteran instructor—one who has experience in conducting the specific training sessions and who knows the subject matter. The non-scripted approach enables this instructor, like Dan, to stick to the "game plan," and at the same time allows enough freedom to personally stylize the session.

Non-Scripted from the Ground Up

Perhaps the best way to get a feel for a non-scripted Session Plan is to build one from the ground up. Just as you can't learn to drive a car without actually sitting behind the wheel and driving, you can't learn about Session Plans by reading a book about them. You have to roll up your sleeves and write the Session Plan.

For the next few minutes, assume you are preparing a non-scripted Session Plan for kindergarten teachers to use in teaching their students shoe-tying. Naturally, there are many considerations and factors involved, but for the purpose of this example, a general approach will suffice. In addition, the approach outlined in this Session Plan is not the only way for kindergarten children to learn to tie shoes. However, the subject matter for this Session Plan is really not of any concern; the Session Plan itself is the true focal point of the discussion.

Since this Session Plan will be directed toward experienced instructors, to allow them maximum flexibility within a given framework, even single words can compose the Session Plan. The word "introduction," for example, would probably be all right for openers, except that it is very general and trite. How about something a little more specific? Considering the age of the audience and what would be effective with that particular group, what about something like "Why"? Like this:

Shoe-Tying

Step 1 ... Why

Here's an opportunity for the experienced teacher to "sell" the kids on why knowing how to tie their shoes is advantageous. Some of the points the instructor might want to cover under this heading include emphasizing that shoe-tying is something the children can do themselves, without any help from mom and dad, brother and sister. The teacher might also want to motivate the children by explaining to them how much of an impression they can make by demonstrating their newly-learned skill.

With just a few key words, then, in the beginning of a non-scripted Session Plan, you can cue the user to cover all of the above points. Here's one way the session plan might appear:

Shoe-Tying

Step 1 ... Why
   — Do yourself
   — Impress

All teachers who use this non-scripted Session Plan would provide essentially uniform instruction, since it covers virtually the same ground. An additional advantage of this type of Session Plan is that it allows the teachers a certain amount of elbow room to cover their material. Even though they would eventually discuss all of the above points, the Session Plan users could cover them in a different order and in a different depth. Notice that the non-scripted Session Plan doesn't necessarily provide guidelines for sequence and for amount of detail. (These constraints could, of course, be incorporated into both non-scripted and scripted Session Plans at the instructor's option.)

Now, let's build the next single-word block of the non-scripted Session Plan. After the introduction, some sort of general explanation of the procedure for tying shoes is in order. What could be a better heading than "general explanation"? It signals, in two words, the teacher to proceed with a review of what the successful shoe tier does first, second, third, and fourth. For example:

Shoe-Tying

Step 2 . . . General explanation

Step 2 in the Session Plan differs from Step 1 by providing a more structured sequence of items for the teacher to cover. Here there are fewer options. The instructor can freely select the depth and amount of detail to use, but he or she has much less freedom in reviewing the actual sequence of tying shoes. Of course, if there is an optional sequence, it can always be written into the Session Plan. In this portion of the non-scripted session plan (as well as the scripted and combination Session Plans) there is a relatively rigid order in which the teacher is to present the necessary information. Here's how the Session Plan might reflect that order:

Shoe-Tying

Step 2 . . . General explanation
    — Cross
    — Knot

— Loop #1
— Loop #2
— Tighten

The non-scripted Session Plan on shoe-tying is beginning to take form and substance. After the children have been properly introduced to the topic and seemingly motivated to learn about it, and after they've received a general explanation of the procedure involved in tying shoes, the next step is for the audience to practice their newly-learned skill so that they can become proficient at it. In the non-scripted Session Plan for shoe-tying, then, Step 3 would consist of a practice period, and might be labeled in the actual Session Plan as follows:

Shoe-Tying

Step 3 . . . Try?

The teacher would perceive this step in the Session Plan as an excellent opportunity to introduce a practice session or workshop *if* the children were ready for it. The question mark, which is a typical shorthand notation found in many non-scripted Session Plans, telegraphs that this step is optional. If the children are prepared and anxious to practice shoe-tying, the Session Plan indicates that this would be a perfect opportunity to do so. On the other hand, if the youngsters are bored, disinterested, or tired, they wouldn't necessarily practice shoe-tying at this point. Again, in the true spirit of non-scripted Session Plans, the teacher could use his or her own judgment. Perhaps a repeat of Steps 1 and 2 is in order. Maybe a simple review of everything covered up to this point would be good. Or perhaps it would be best to forget it altogether and just start again another day. In any event, the choice, indicated by the simple question mark in the non-scripted Session Plan, is the teacher's to make.

If the teacher decides to go ahead with the practice period, the non-scripted Session Plan outlines the way to proceed. To reiterate, the non-scripted Session Plan provides a general guideline but leaves the depth and sequence of coverage up to the instructor. Of course, there are many conceivable ways to conduct practice sessions, but in this example, the Session Plan sets forth this method: First, the teacher demonstrates, stage by stage, exactly how to tie a pair of shoelaces. Second, everyone in the class practices all of the different stages, from crossing to knotting, to making the first and second loops, and to tightening. In this stage, the class is still following the teacher's example. Third, each person in the class, individually and without the teacher's example, practices each stage. Fourth, and finally, everyone practices all the different stages, all the way through, without the benefit of demonstration by the instructor.

A non-scripted Session Plan on shoe-tying would possibly describe the above practice period, in all of its detail, in a very simple shorthand.

Shoe-Tying

Step 3 . . . Try?
    — Step by step (with me)
    — All together (with me)
    — Step by step (alone)
    — All together (alone)

The non-scripted shoe-tying session plan would conclude by spelling out an abbreviated review procedure. It might be headed this way:

Shoe-Tying

Step 4 . . . Review

Unlike the practice period outlined in Step 3, Step 4 is a *must*. Therefore, the non-scripted Session Plan contains no symbols, like the question mark, indicating that the instructor has a choice. However, within the confines of the review itself, there is considerable opportunity for flexibility of participants, depth, and sequence. For example, the teacher could call on volunteers to conduct the review, or the teacher could lead it. Since peer instruction is effective in teaching shoe-tying, asking for volunteers would be a good technique. The volunteers could conduct the review period by repeating the instruction and then by holding another practice workshop. Here's how a non-scripted Session Plan on shoe-tying would document the entire review step:

Shoe-Tying

Step 4 . . . Review
 — Volunteers?
 — Repeat
 — Practice

Again, the objective here is for the non-scripted Session Plan to convey a plan for covering a teaching or training session without going into elaborate detail. Such important considerations as time limits and approaches, such as using volunteers, are up to the discretion of the teacher and are communicated by punctuation marks (Volunteers?) or even by deletion (time limits).

To summarize, here is the entire non-scripted Session Plan for shoe-tying:

Shoe-Tying

Step 1 . . . Why
 — Do yourself
 — Impress

Step 2 . . . General explanation
   — Cross
   — Knot
   — Loop #1
   — Loop #2
   — Tighten

Step 3 . . . Try?
   — Step by Step (with me)
   — All together (with me)
   — Step by step (alone)
   — All together (alone)

Step 4 . . . Review
   — Volunteers?
   — Repeat
   — Practice

The important point to remember about writing non-scripted Session Plans, whether they're for school or for business, is to keep them simple and clear for comprehensive, yet flexible, instruction.

Scripted Session Plans

The opposite technique of preparing non-scripted Session Plans is developing scripted Session Plans. Unlike a non-scripted Session Plan, a scripted Session Plan is usually written in complete sentences; it doesn't provide much room for freedom and deviation. However, the scripted Session Plan is intended for an inexperienced instructor, or for one who has to learn his or her subject matter in a short time. In fact, the scripted Session Plan is really a step-by-step method of training the trainer to train his or her class.

Scripted vs. Non-Scripted Session Plans

Figure 5 outlines the differences between scripted and non-scripted Session Plans. Before we analyze a scripted Session Plan, let's see how it relates to a non-scripted Session

Figure 5

Non-Scripted Session Plan vs. Scripted Session Plan

Non-Scripted	Scripted
1. Written in sentence fragments	1. Written in complete sentences
2. Plenty of room for flexibility	2. Not much room for flexibility
3. Intended for experienced instructor	3. Intended for inexperienced instructor
4. Cannot be read verbatim	4. Can practically be read as is, if necessary
5. Requires considerable additional development	5. Requires little, if any, additional development

Plan. A scripted Session Plan, for example, is almost always written in complete sentences. In fact, some scripted Session Plans are even used as scripts, with the inexperienced instructor actually reading them verbatim. Complete sentences are a limitation for experienced instructors, since they frequently prefer to inject a certain amount of tailoring and customizing into their training classes. For the new and inexperienced trainers, however, scripted Session Plans with complete sentences are an excellent method of providing information and instilling confidence. If a scripted Session Plan locks an experienced instructor in, it opens up new vistas to the inexperienced teachers.

Not having room for flexibility is advantageous in some situations, especially when an instructor is new or if there is a last-minute change of instructors without adequate time for the new trainer to adequately prepare for his or her session. Most uninitiated instructors aren't eager to improvise at first. Their primary concern is doing as well as possible in a new and different environment and making the best possible impression. There is plenty of time later for trial and error. For these people, a scripted Session Plan is simply a track to run on. Assuming it is the right track, the session will come off well. Students aren't likely to notice the difference between the amateurs and the pros, at least as far as the subject matter material is concerned.

The reason why scripted Session Plans are intended primarily for the inexperienced instructor is because they provide total guidance. By definition, a person without any knowledge whatever about either training or subject matter should be able to pick up a scripted Session Plan and use it immediately without the slightest preparation. The inexperienced trainer or educator should be able to conduct the session effectively and lead the class in such a way that it accomplishes its objectives. This trainer may be dissatisfied with some of the fine points of his or her instruction and may want to refine it accordingly; the scripted Session Plan doesn't promise perfection. What it does do is lead the teacher by the hand down a clear-cut path to accomplishing the session's objectives. The novice instructor may stumble along the way, but he'll get there in the end.

One of the definite advantages of scripted Session Plans is that they can be read verbatim. Reading anything out loud, as a "canned" presentation, is certainly not a very effective or impressive method of communication. It comes across as boring, monotonous, stilted, irrelevant, and at best, discourteous and unprepared. A Session Plan, particularly, since it is supposed to effect learning, should be a model of professional communication and should rarely, if ever, be actually read. A scripted Session Plan, however, can be so effectively paraphrased, with a minimum of preparation, that the new or last-minute replacement trainer comes across as an expert. Best of all, the scripted Session Plan by definition includes specific explanations of visuals and all other graphics and materials designed to supplement a particular training session. By closely following both the text and notes in a scripted Session Plan, even an inexperienced instructor on Day One of Session One can accomplish the desired objectives, and, at the same time, come off as a training pro.

Finally, a true scripted Plan requires no additional development or refinement. It's ready to use, the moment a trainer picks it up and looks at it for the first time. Every trainer, however, regardless of his or her experience level, must prepare for a training session based on a scripted Session Plan, just as he or she would prepare to teach a class that will follow a non-scripted Session Plan. These types of preparations include assembling handout material, organizing slides and other audio-visual materials, developing flip sheets, reserving and arranging training rooms, and alerting participants to the time, place, and location of their training class. All of these preparations, however, are not actually a part of the scripted Session Plan. The only adjustment that a scripted Session Plan requires is updating. If the subject matter covered by the scripted Session Plan changes and becomes obsolete, the information involved will need to be changed. The training techniques, organization, and approach, however, which are the main ingredients of all Session Plans—scripted, non-scripted, or combination—should require no change. The scripted Session Plan, particularly, should stand on its own, independent of additional input from the user.

Having compared a non-scripted Session Plan with a scripted version, the next step is to examine a typical scripted Session Plan to distinguish the five features explained above. Figure 6 illustrates a portion of a typical scripted Session Plan.

A Typical Scripted Session Plan

Notice that the scripted Session Plan is written in complete sentences. More importantly, it is scripted. In other words, it is designed so that an instructor can read it verbatim, and at the same time, cover his or her teaching points. The example is relatively inflexible; it doesn't provide room for deviation. In fact, the trainer's only real opportunity to expand on the topic is at the very beginning, when he or she is leading a discussion of how the XYZ Insurance Company uses the different codes. But from that point on, the teacher is tied to the Session Plan. As pointed out previously, such inflexibility has several advantages; the Session Plan is highly structured in order to provide maximum direction and guidance for inexperienced instructors. Finally, the sample scripted Session Plan illustrated in Figure 6 requires very little, if any, additional fine-tuning before it can be used. Virtually any

Figure 6

Portion of a Scripted Session Plan

EXHIBITS (FORMS/SLIDES)	OUTLINE
SLIDE 4-2	II. Discuss how the XYZ Insurance Company uses each of the following codes:

A. *Coverage Codes*—record the specific kinds of protection that we sell to our customers. For example, in the case of auto insurance, we provide coverage (protection) for such things as bodily injury, property damage, collision, etc. Also, any special treatments, such as the application of limits and deductibles, must be statistically recorded. We collect all this information so that we can ultimately analyze how our loss experience compares with premiums charged.

new instructor can pick it up and run with it at a moment's notice. This assumes, of course, that all of the basic teacher preparations have been completed. But the scripted Session Plan should require no additional scripting, editing, or re-working. It is designed to be ready for instant use.

Combination Session Plans

Before moving on, it is important to realize that the difference between non-scripted and scripted Session Plans is definitely not always as clear-cut as in the above examples. There is such a thing as a combination of the two types of session plans. In fact, if we take a look at the introductory portion of the previous example, which now is labeled Figure 7, we can see an excellent illustration of a combination non-scripted and scripted Session Plan.

The combination plan is perhaps the most frequently written Session Plan. It features the best of what the non-scripted and scripted Session Plans offer, and combines them in an extremely workable format, which can be tailored to fit any teacher. In Figure 7, the combination technique is applied to its best advantage. The introductory portion, in Roman numeral I, is non-scripted. If a new trainer is going to adopt a loosely-structured approach, the introduction is the place to do it. The remainder of the combination plan is complex. A new instructor would be uncomfortable and ineffective with a loosely constructed Session Plan here. Therefore, a scripted Session Plan is used, since it provides good direction and guidance. The blend of the two teaching styles—free and loose in the beginning, direct and to the point in the subject matter coverage—helps the teacher to be relaxed yet confident, thus hopefully effecting the desired learning.

Summary of Three Kinds of Session Plans

To summarize briefly, all Session Plans are written in one

Figure 7

*Combination Scripted and
Non-Scripted Session Plan*

EXHIBITS (FORMS/SLIDES) OUTLINE

SLIDE 4-1

I. Explain what specific codes will be discussed in today's Workshop session

  A. Coverage Codes

    1. Coverage

    2. Deductible

    3. Limits

    4. Line — Sub-Line

SLIDE 4-2

II. Discuss how the XYZ Insurance Company uses each of the following codes:

  A. *Coverage Codes*—record the specific kinds of protection that we sell to our customers. For example, in the case of auto insurance, we provide coverage (protection) for such things as bodily injury, property damage, collision, etc. Also, any special treatments, such as the application of limits and deductibles, must be statistically recorded. We collect all this information so that we can ultimately analyze how our loss experience compares with premiums charged.

of three styles: non-scripted, scripted, or a combination of the two. But no matter which of these three writing styles is used to construct a Session Plan, every Session Plan consists of four main parts: *introduction, procedure, practice,* and *wrap-up.* Let's now take a look at each of these four main parts in detail, and then put them all together to see how they compose a typical Session Plan.

The Introduction

The introduction is extremely important because it sets the stage for the entire session. If the introduction is poorly planned, it jeopardizes what follows. Since all three kinds of Session Plans, non-scripted, scripted, and combination, should contain an introduction, let's take a close look to see how it can be worded.

Non-Scripted Introduction. A non-scripted introduction is illustrated in Figure 8. Even a simple, basic introduction like this serves four critical needs of all training sessions. First, the introduction reminds the trainer or teacher to welcome the trainees and to loosen up any inhibitions they may be feeling. In the case of a non-scripted introduction, the actual directions for how to welcome the trainees to the session are not provided, but certainly the suggestion is there. The rest is up to the trainer, which again is why the non-scripted Session Plan is best used by the experienced teacher. With the introduction in Figure 8 as a starting point, it is conceivable that every teacher who uses it would proceed differently. For example, one trainer might decide to incorporate a sophisticated introduction by suggesting that the students split up into groups of two each. In this method, the two partners interview each other thoroughly enough to obtain certain key facts: names, reasons for attending the training class, and interests. Then the partners reconvene in a large group session, in which all the partners take turns introducing each

Figure 8

Introduction Section of a Non-Scripted Session Plan

I. Introduction and welcome
   A. What
   B. Why
   C. Terminology

other to the rest of the group. Another trainer, on the other hand, might take an entirely different approach. He or she could conceivably handle introductions by personally introducing each participant. The instructor could even eliminate introductions altogether and leave this aspect of the training session to the trainees to take care of on their own during coffee breaks, lunches, or other informal gatherings. In other words, a non-scripted introduction is used as a welcoming device. As such, it can be administered in any of at least three different styles, depending on the trainer's preference.

A non-scripted introduction serves a second need of all training sessions. The introducton provides the teacher or trainer with an excellent opportunity to review the session's objectives. Again with reference to Figure 8, objectives would fit in under the topic "what." This is where the trainer would review what areas the training class is going to cover. Although this particular non-scripted Session Plan doesn't specifically mention them, this would be a natural point for an astute teacher to review expected outcomes. As in welcoming the trainees, with a non-scripted introduction, the instructor would review the objectives of the training session in his or her own way. For example, the more obvious and direct method of presenting objectives to a training class is simply to explain them, straight out, at the beginning of the session. Another, more subtle and perhaps more interesting method of covering objectives is to skip over them—at the beginning of the class. But when the session is finished, the trainer reveals the objectives that he or she has written ahead of time and hidden on the chalkboard or on a flip sheet. This second method of covering objectives is more impactful than the first method because it is relatively easy for the trainees to compare actual outcomes at the end of the course with the instructor's objectives. To reiterate a point made earlier, a non-scripted Session Plan has a flexibility advantage over a scripted or even a combination Plan, at least for an experienced, knowledgeable teacher.

Third, a non-scripted introduction usually includes an informative overview of the session to follow. The overview, most of which would also fall under "what" in Figure 8, is a natural extension of the objectives. However, again using this Session Plan's flexibility to his or her advantage, a perceptive teacher may want to reverse this order and cover the overview first, to present "the big picture," and follow that with a specific statement of objectives. Another point of interest in the sample non-scripted introduction in Figure 8, is that a review of basic terminology could nicely be included in the overview.

Finally, and most importantly, a non-scripted introduction serves as a signpost to the instructor to explain the reasoning behind the session topic: *why* a certain procedure is performed, or *why* a given report is necessary. This rationale will motivate the trainees, and hopefully get them involved in the presentation. Figure 8 illustrates how the rationale can be covered following the objectives and overview. However, an imaginative teacher might elect to make a special point of why the training is being conducted, and therefore might decide to put the rationale at the top of the session. All of the other points to be covered in the introduction would then follow. Or there may be certain advantages for saving the rationale until the finale of the introduction. For example, the teacher may want to be sure his or her class hits the subject matter on an upbeat. Certainly, a non-scripted introduction encourages such flexibility.

Scripted Introduction. But what about the introduction in a scripted Session Plan? Since non-scripted and scripted Session Plans differ so drastically, do their introductions differ as well? To answer this question, look now at Figure 9, which represents the introduction section of a scripted

Figure 9

Introduction Section of a Scripted Session Plan

Welcome to the Telephone Training Workshop. Since we all had an opportunity to get to know one another at last evening's get-together, we can move ahead with today's session.

Let's look at how we can use our telephone system efficiently. We'll review what our telephone system's features are, and we'll review how you can use each of these features. Although our phone system is complex in design, its actual use is very simple, and the skills you need to use the system are easily mastered.

Incidentally, feel free to ask questions if you don't fully understand something we cover. At certain points in our review, you'll have opportunities to practice using various telephone features.

Session Plan. This introduction accomplishes just about what the non-scripted introduction accomplishes in Figure 8, but with a completely different approach.

The scripted introduction in Figure 9 leads with a basic welcome. It is obviously not a formal welcome, because this has already been handled. But the session does include a reference to a welcome that is actually "scripted" into the training class, which officially began "last evening." In the telephone training class, the introduction served as an ice-breaker; whatever inhibitions the trainees were feeling have already been loosened up.

The scripted introduction also reviews the objectives of the training session and then provides an overview of the session. These points are covered in the second paragraph. Finally, the scripted introduction provides the proper motivation by emphasizing the relative simplicity of the telephone and by assuring the trainees that they'll have plenty of opportunity, later in the session, to practice their newly-learned skills.

There is, of course, one basic, important difference between the two introductions featured in Figures 8 and 9. The difference is degree of flexibility. Using the introduction in Figure 8, the instructor has considerable freedom. He or she can vary both the sequence and the depth of the introduction. The introduction in Figure 9, however, is different; it is designed to be read rather than interpreted or paraphrased. The sequence and depth are predetermined.

Combination Introduction. For another view of an introduction section of a Session Plan, look now at Figure 10. It is an example of an introduction to a typical combination Session Plan. It, too, contains the key elements of an introduction, but communicates them uniquely.

There is one key element, however, which is missing from this particular Session Plan. There is no welcome as such. Whoever prepared this Session Plan assumed that the user

Figure 10

Introduction Section of a Combination Session Plan

1. *Introduction*

   (1)   Explain the reason for conducting this training session

   (2)   Explain the objectives of this session by reviewing the Training
         Objectives Section of this Module with the trainees

   (3)   Distribute handouts. Explain their purpose and how to use
         them
         — Outline of important information
         — Ready reference
         — Supplemental information

   (4)   Review the key elements of this Module, briefly highlighting
         the topics that will be covered

would simply realize that an "icebreaker" of some type was necessary and would include it on his or her own. The point in the introduction where the welcome would normally come is open-ended. This is a combination Session Plan, and the welcome is non-scripted; as a matter of fact, it is not even included.

The second key element of a combination introduction is represented in Figure 10. The example clearly guides the trainer through a thorough review of the training objectives before the session begins. In fact, the training material referenced in this particular example even contains a special "Training Objectives Section."

Figure 10 also illustrates an example of an informative overview, which is the third critical component of a Session Plan introduction. In addition, the illustration makes mention of the reasoning behind the session topic. Since this is one of the most important elements of the introduction portion of a Session Plan, it appears at the very beginning of the Session Plan, right where the trainer is certain to see it.

Like the non-scripted and scripted Session Plans, then, the combination plan includes an introduction, which usually consists of four parts: welcome, objectives, overview, and rationale. Occasionally, one or more of these key ingredients may be missing from the introduction, but as a rule, they are all included.

The Procedure

The second of the four essential parts of a Session Plan is the procedure, which usually follows the introduction. All three types of Session Plans—non-scripted, scripted, and combination—feature a procedure section. The procedure involves an explanation, using examples, of what the subject of the Session Plan is: how it's done, who does it, and when and where it's done. The procedure is the heart of the entire

Session Plan; it is the reason for the training in the first place. The three other major parts of the Session Plan merely reinforce and drive home what's contained in the procedure.

Non-Scripted Procedure. Beginning with the non-scripted Session Plan, in Figure 11, let's look at one way to prepare the procedure section. This example outlines the theoretical steps that an instructor might review with a beginning developer of training programs and materials in the training department in business or industry. Adhering to the criteria for a non-scripted Session Plan, this example of the procedure section presents the steps to be followed in the order in which they are to be followed. The introductory section of this Session Plan, not illustrated here, has set up the procedure and, assuming the instructor administered the introduction properly, the class is ready to get on with the subject matter. Since the procedure section is non-scripted, the instructor will hopefully apply his or her knowledge, experience, and creativity in getting the message across. There is, however, little of the same opportunity for flexibility in the procedure that there is in the introduction. The steps to be taught are clear and precise; they are to be followed in the proper sequence. But certainly there is room for considerable amplification. The trainer will expand on each of the points covered in the procedure until he or she feels that the material has been covered adequately and that the students are prepared to demonstrate their new knowledge. In addition, this example of a typical procedure section offers opportunity for the experienced instructor to use appropriate, effective transitions between points in the outline. There is also plenty of room here for exhibits and personal anecdotes and experiences.

In other words, in this example, and in the example of the non-scripted introduction (Figure 8), the class is almost totally dependent on instructor or peer input. The only

Figure 11

Procedure Section of a Non-Scripted Session Plan

III. Developing a training program

    A. Needs analysis

    B. Objectives

    C. Proposal

    D. Research

    E. Writing
       1. First draft
       2. Final draft

    F. Approval

    G. Production

    H. Distribution

    I. Evaluation

structure provided is in the organization and sequence of the subject matter. Qualified, imaginative teachers would have a "field day" with this session. It is simple to understand why new or inexperienced teachers, however, would prefer to use either a scripted or at least a combination approach.

Scripted Procedure. To take the procedure noted in Figure 11 one step further, let's see how it would appear in scripted format in Figure 12. This is simply an expansion of the outline in Figure 11; space does not permit a completed example of this scripted Session Plan, but its scope should be evident. Regardless of the amount of detail, the scripted procedure is the central point of the training session. It features the same criteria as the non-scripted procedure illustrated in Figure 11.

Combination Procedure. Finally, in Figure 13, we can see how the procedure section of a combination Session Plan compares with the examples of procedure sections of scripted and non-scripted Session Plans. Again, the content is identical to the subject matter illustrated in Figures 11 and 12, but the format of the procedure is developed differently, in keeping with the general guidelines for combination session plans reviewed previously.

In retrospect, then, the procedure section is the second of four essential parts of a session plan. The first main part is the introduction. Whether the Session Plan is non-scripted, scripted, or a combination of both formats, the procedure section plays the same role. It is the core, the meat, of the training session itself. The three other essential parts, which include the introduction, practice, and wrap-up sections, simply augment and highlight the procedure. Without the procedure, there is no reason to have the training in the first place.

The Practice

With a thorough understanding of the first half of a typical Session Plan in mind, the next step is to discuss the practice section. Many times, particularly as the number of sessions in a course proliferate and as time grows short, there is a tendency to complete the impartation of information at the expense of practice, or hands-on training. A well-documented Session Plan can at least serve the purpose of reminding the trainer to include some practice time. The Session Plan can indicate how much time should be spent practicing, and what to do to practice most effectively. Typical practice exercises include filling in blank forms, playing roles, or simply repeating statements.

Non-Scripted Practice. Perhaps the best way to see how beneficial the practice section can be is to return to an example of a non-scripted Session Plan, which Figure 14 depicts. The format of a non-scripted session is certainly a familiar sight by now. With brief notes as guidelines, an experienced trainer could use this part of his or her session plan to lead a class in practicing the process of actual Addressograph work items. The trainer provides all of the elaboration required, fills in the blanks, and establishes the transitions between the steps of the practice session.

By the time they proceed to the practice section, the participants in this particular training session have received all of the necessary theory, background, and motivation for processing Addressograph work items. The trainers have also received some education about the required procedure. If the Session Plan were to end here, however, the trainees would leave without having had the very valuable opportunity to practice their theory and procedure; they probably wouldn't be able to perform as expected on the job. With practice, however, the participants in this Addressograph training workshop are able to master the principles. As they

Figure 14

Practice Section of a Non-Scripted Session Plan

(1) Work sample selection

(2) Distribution and instruction; demonstration if necessary

(3) Assistance

(4) Amount of practice

(5) Spotcheck and correction

(6) Release

practice, they receive the necessary feedback and reinforcement. These consequences will guide them to the correct procedure and will enable them to apply their newly learned techniques when they handle real Addressograph items after they leave the training session.

In this example, the trainer is furnished with a game plan for conducting an effective practice session. Here, as in previous examples of the non-scripted format, which have already been presented, there is room for flexibility and adjustment, depending on how the trainer sees the needs of the trainees. A non-scripted practice section is less open to interpretation than a non-scripted introduction because in the practice, the sequence is more critical. If the practice section doesn't proceed according to plan, the desired outcome may not occur. It's much easier and less damaging to adjust the order of the points covered in the introduction. The extent of any of the practice phases, however, should be carefully adjusted and fine tuned by the experienced instructor. Frequently, the extent and duration of a practice session will depend on the trainees themselves and their degree of prior knowledge and skill.

Often, the first two sections of the Session Plan are administered so successfully and with so few questions and problems that there is little need for any practice. Just as often, on the other hand, the reverse is true. The best way to tell how long the practice section will last is to begin it. An experienced trainer will be able to distinguish between trainees who need extensive practice and those who need only a single run-through.

Scripted Practice. Having reviewed a non-scripted practice section, let's see how a scripted practice section compares. An illustration of a practice section of a scripted session plan appears in Figure 15. The scripted version, as usual, provides all the information required. All the trainer has to do is

Figure 15

Practice Section of a Scripted Session Plan

To get the proper feel of processing actual work items, let's spend a few minutes practicing the procedure we've just reviewed.

(1) I've selected a number of new business, endorsement, renewal, and cancellation/termination work samples, plus some samples of the various lists processed in our unit. I should emphasize that these are "live" items, not just mock-ups specially prepared for you to practice with.

(2) I'm going to distribute the work samples now. As soon as you've received your material and had a chance to look it over, I'll explain how to start processing the work items. If anything's unclear or if you have any questions, be sure to let me know right away. If you'd like me to, I'll walk you through the first few items ...

follow along; there is very little adjustment required from class to class. Whether the practice section is non-scripted or scripted, however, the objective is to provide trainees with involvement; to let them see what happens when they apply their new knowledge and skills to "live" situations. The ultimate goal, of course, is for the practice period to be a successful transfer agent between the classroom and the job. The more closely the practice simulates "real world" conditions, the more likely the possibility of the training taking effect and holding.

Combination Practice. For a final look at a possible format for the practice section of a Session Plan, look now at Figure 16. This is an example of the practice section of a combination Session Plan. Little explanation is required here, except to say that this example meets the criteria of the combination introduction and procedure sections reviewed earlier. The objective of the practice session outlined here is exactly the same as the objective of the non-scripted and scripted versions: Provide the trainees with an opportunity to practice their Addressograph processing skills so that they can apply them successfully when they return to their desks at the conclusion of training.

To summarize briefly, whether it is formatted in non-scripted, scripted, or combination format, the practice section of a Session Plan helps the trainees make a transition from the world of theory to the world of reality. It is so simple to sit in a training session and feel that the information presented there is appropriate, whereas it might actually be totally unuseable. A substantive practice period bridges the gap between what looks good on paper and what really works. How a trainer administers the practice depends on the type of Session Plan he or she selects.

Figure 16

Practice Section of a Combination Session Plan

Conduct a practice session to enable trainees to get the feel of processing actual work items:

- Select a number of new business, endorsement, renewal, and cancellation/termination work samples as well as some samples of the various lists processed in our unit.

- Distribute the work among the trainees and instruct them on how to start processing the work samples. You may have to step them all the way through the first few items.

- Remain in the area to offer any assistance that the trainees may need.

- Provide as much practice as you feel is necessary to bring the performance of the trainees to an adequate level.

- Spotcheck all the work and have the trainees correct their errors.

- Release the work only after it has been corrected.

The Wrap-Up

The fourth of four essential parts of a Session Plan is the wrap-up section. Here is an opportunity to conclude the training with a fresh, clear, and meaningful impression in the mind of the trainee. When the learner leaves the classroom, the training goes right along, just as you researched it, planned it, and administered it. But if the wrap-up is poor, or non-existent, trainees may not take your message along; at best, they may confuse or garble it. So don't take chances—you have worked too hard and your mission is too important. Let the wrap-up put the finishing touches on your training session. Good, solid wrap-up activities are quizzes and question-and-answer sessions.

Non-Scripted Wrap-Up. Figure 17 presents one example of a wrap-up section of a non-scripted Session Plan. This example reflects the usual characteristics of non-scripted Session Plans and is administered most effectively by a qualified, experienced trainer. This wrap-up is extremely flexible, both in depth and in sequence. A knowledgeable trainer could implement the wrap-up in a variety of sequences, spend varying lengths of time on each portion, and establish tailored transitions from one topic to another.

Scripted Wrap-Up. In Figure 18, a scripted version of a wrap-up is presented. Here, the trainer can simply read the Session Plan as it is.

Combination Wrap-Up. Finally, Figure 19 depicts a wrap-up section of a combination session plan. It can't be read verbatim like its cousin, the scripted wrap-up, but it does provide more guidance and direction than a non-scripted wrap-up.

Summary

The Design Format section has presented, analyzed, and illustrated the four essential parts of non-scripted, scripted,

Figure 17

Wrap-Up Section of a Non-Scripted Session Plan

19. Wrap-up

(1) Content summary

(2) Performance standards

(3) Questions

(4) Review test

Figure 18

Wrap-Up Section of a Scripted Session Plan

19. Now let's be sure we have a satisfactory understanding of the information contained in this Module.

    (1) I think we can best accomplish this objective by first summarizing the Module content.

    (2) Then we can review the performance standards expected of an experienced individual who performs the functions covered in our training class. These standards aren't applicable now, however, because you've just completed your training. Rather, these performance standards will be expected of you only after you've had considerable on-the-job experience.

    (3) Then, if you have any questions, we'll stop and answer them if at all possible.

    (4) Finally, you'll have an opportunity to test your knowledge of the material we've covered today, and to obtain some feedback on your performance in a simulated desk-level environment, by taking a special review test. We'll go over the answers to the review test immediately after you complete the test.

Figure 19

Wrap-Up Section of a Combination Session Plan

19. Be sure that all trainees have a satisfactory understanding of the information contained in this Module.

   (1) Summarize the content of this Module.

   (2) Review the performance standards expected of an experienced individual who performs the functions just covered. Explain that these are the standards that will be expected of the trainees after they have had considerable on-the-job experience.

   (3) Ask the trainees if they have any question and, if so, provide answers.

   (4) Administer the Review Test
       — After you grade the answers to the Review Test, go over the results with the trainees.

and combination Session Plans. To summarize briefly, the non-scripted Session Plan is only a guide. It points experienced trainers in the right direction, but it doesn't lead them by the hand. It is written in sentence fragments, and could conceivably require substantial shoring up with research, additional information, and expansion before it could be used. But it is flexible, and as such is excellent for decentralized trainee audiences with extensive local differentiation from standard practice and procedure.

The scripted Session Plan paints the complete picture; it is written in complete sentences. In fact, is it so complete and self-contained, the trainer could even read it verbatim.

The combination Session Plan simply merges the non-scripted and scripted approaches. Although the combination Session Plan employs complete sentences, it provides only the framework, like a sentence outline. The teacher or trainer receives guidance from a combination Session Plan, but can still follow a flexible method of presenting material to his or her class.

Finally, the Design Format section has described the four essential parts of a Session Plan. They are the introduction, procedure, practice, and wrap-up.

The introduction sets up the entire session. The procedure explains how the job is done. In the practice part of a Session Plan, trainees have a chance to get their hands on the job; to learn by experiencing either the real thing or a simulation. And the wrap-up reinforces the introduction, procedure, and practice by reviewing them.

Non-scripted, scripted, and combination Session Plans usually comprise all four essential parts, as the Figures in the Design Format section have illustrated.

IV.

OUTCOMES

All three kinds of Session Plans, which this book has presented, described, and illustrated, benefit everyone who is affected by them. Specifically, Session Plans have advantages for both students and teachers. In addition, Session Plans have several administrative and organizational benefits. Let's begin by reviewing the benefits a student receives by attending classes taught by instructors who use Session Plans.

Student Advantages

The primary purpose of a Session Plan, whether nonscripted, scripted, or combination, is to organize instruction. A Session Plan accomplishes this objective with its four essential parts, which consist of an introduction, procedure, practice, and wrap-up.

Organized instruction, communicated in clear, simple Session Plan format, and presented according to the Session Plan, affects the learning process by enabling students to absorb, comprehend, and remember the subject matter.

Numerous studies and years of experience testify to the correlation between organization and learning. Psychologists recognize that material which is both highly meaningful and highly organized is more easily learned than material which has low meaning and which is unorganized.

Another advantage for students who receive information via Session Plans is uniformity of instruction. If, for example, three different teachers all use the same Session Plan, their students should receive essentially the same message. The Session Plans, of course, do allow for individualism, flexibility, and tailoring, but also contribute a unifying factor to the instruction.

Session Plans also help ensure that a trainee's classroom time is used to its maximum potential. A class that is well planned and documented will usually be organized, with literally every minute, or at least every quarter hour, accounted for. There is a minimum of time left, and, as a result, more is accomplished than if the time were unstructured.

What about the student's reaction to all of this detailed planning? Usually, the trainee reacts favorably. Students appreciate the extra effort their teachers go through to prepare meaningful classes. Even if a student never sees the Session Plan, or knows it exists, he or she will recognize the teacher's professionalism that becomes evident as a result of using a Session Plan. Students who are impressed by a teacher's ability are motivated to learn. They also sell their peers on their teacher and on instruction in general.

Finally, trainees whose trainers rely on Session Plans will receive updated information if the instructors properly revise their Session Plans. Subject matter that is documented in Session Plan format can easily be updated, which provides students with up-to-the-minute information. Trainees don't have to rely on heresay, assumption, or the grapevine to get their facts straight.

Benefits for Teachers

Teachers and instructors benefit even more than trainees or organizations by using Session Plans. Teachers, like students, find organization advantageous. An efficient, effective Session Plan is a key to organization. With a Session Plan, a teacher is in control; the session runs according to plan, not by accident or by circumstances beyond the teacher's control. Controlled instruction, incidentally, is not synonymous with non-participative training. Instruction laid out and documented in approved Session Plan format can be *planned* as involvement-oriented as easily as it can be *planned* to come across as more highly structured and authoritarian. The key is *planning*, with the teacher or trainer, not the student, at the controls.

In addition, a well-planned training class, based on a Session Plan, will usually succeed even with technical and content inaccuracies. An unplanned session, on the other hand, which is *ad-libbed* at the instructor's whim, will probably fail, even if the instruction is completely error-free. This success/failure formula is true largely because of the human element. Teachers who use Session Plans come across to students as being competent and professional. These teachers "sell" their products, whereas unprepared trainers, whom trainees recognize as being para-professionals at best, don't adequately communicate with the trainees and therefore sometimes lose the battle before they even fire a single shot.

Another advantage for teachers who use Session Plans is that there is a plan for every teacher's experience level. Regardless of whether a trainer is experienced, inexperienced, or somewhere in between, he or she can capitalize on the appropriate type of Session Plan. Experienced teachers can identify with non-scripted Session Plans, inexperienced trainers prefer scripted Session Plans, and teachers with some experience can use combination Session Plans.

Session Plans also help trainers, instructors, and teachers utilize their time most efficiently. Even non-scripted Session Plans, which frequently don't note the recommended amount of time to spend on any aspect of a training class, help trainers organize their time by outlining all of the areas to be covered within a certain class. The teacher is free to spend as much or as little time as required on any of the topics.

Another benefit of this valuable training technique for Session Plan users is reflected in the professionalism of their classes. Teachers and trainers who prepare and use Session Plans *organize* their instruction, which is perceived by recipients as being efficient and effective. Regardless of their experience level, all instructors bring professionalism to their jobs by following Session Plans. These educators are prepared. They are flexible, too, but they follow a basic plan and don't waste either their time or their students' time.

Session Plans also help their users minimize costly wheel-spinning and duplication of effort by serving as a historical record. If Session Plans are prepared and implemented properly, they can be consulted by trainers whenever they are preparing to conduct classes. Trainers can review past successes and failures, select what they feel are the most noteworthy and applicable techniques, and incorporate them in their own Session Plans. In the future, these Session Plans can be used by other trainers for the same purpose.

Teachers and trainers can update their classes simply by making previous Session Plans current. There is no need to develop brand-new Session Plans from scratch.

Finally, creating and developing Session Plans is one method of force-feeding trainers to become more knowledgeable instructors. The steps of planning, researching, writing, and editing Session Plans creates the need for instructors to base their instruction on facts and logic rather than on last-minute guesswork and trial and error.

Administrative and Organizational Benefits

Last, but certainly not least, Session Plans have many useful advantages for organizations. For example, Session Plans enable schools, businesses, and corporations to administer a consistent and controlled curriculum. If Session Plans are prepared and are on file, an administrative coordinator can simply and easily monitor them to be sure they are in keeping with the organization's principles and guidelines. If a problem or ambiguity is detected, it can quickly be brought to the attention of the trainer responsible, a solution can be developed, and the Session Plan can be revised as required.

Session Plans are excellent for use in teacher or trainer training. New teachers can use scripted or combination Session Plans and become proficient with a minimum amount of practice. Even if there is no trainer, or time to train trainers, an inexperienced instructor can learn a class on the job by following the prescribed Session Plan.

Since Session Plans are consistent and provide tangible evidence of how any given class functions, teacher changes due to illness, vacations, and other interruptions, both scheduled and unscheduled, can be made swiftly with a minimum amount of confusion. A substitute teacher needs only a brief advance look at the recommended Session Plan and the class can continue, with about the same high level of instruction as if the regular teacher were there.

Organizations can also use Session Plans to capitalize on the most effective teaching. With a Session Plan as a record, an organization can separate the effective instruction from the ineffective and thereby upgrade the quality of instruction across the board.

Non-scripted and combination Session Plans, in particular, are useful for organizations that comprise vast, decentralized trainee audiences with significantly varying local conditions. For example, if a large company wants to provide basic supervisory instruction for all of its first-line supervisors, whose jobs differ slightly depending on which offices and in which geographical location they work, the basic Session

Figure 20

Advantages of Session Plans

Advantage	Student	Teacher	School/Company
1. Organization	X	X	
2. Uniform instruction	X		
3. Time	X	X	X
4. Positive impression	X		
5. Current information	X	X	X
6. Planning		X	
7. Experience		X	
8. Professionalism	X	X	X
9. Minimal duplication		X	X
10. Force-feeding		X	
11. Consistency			X
12. Teacher training			X
13. Transition			X
14. Effectiveness			X
15. Decentralization			X

Plan could be developed at headquarters. The Session Plan would contain the key points that the company wanted to communicate, but would be general enough for all of the individual offices across the country to add their own teaching points. The new supervisor trainees, then, would all receive essentially the same training, but it could be geared to reflect local conditions and therefore be more appropriate.

Finally, organizations receive the same benefits that session plans furnish both students and teachers. These benefits include time savings, professionalism, reduction of wheel-spinning and duplication, and update convenience.

In conclusion, Figure 20 outlines all the advantages of Session Plans for students, teachers, and organizations.

V.

DEVELOPMENTAL GUIDE

Figure 21 is a combination procedural guide and worksheet model for preparing non-scripted, scripted, and combination Session Plans. The guide recommends a suggested developer for each essential part of all three types of Session Plans and also indicates the sequence in which each part should be developed. Figure 21 also serves as a worksheet for coordinating actual Session Plan preparation.

For example, assume you are one of the instructors in an advanced supervisory training class, and I am responsible for coordinating the preparation of all the Session Plans used by all of the instructors in the course. If one of your presentations is on non-verbal communications (NVC), I would note that title in the far left-hand column of Figure 21, opposite the type of Session Plan you are planning to use. We will assume you are an expert on NVC and that you are very comfortable on your feet with it. Since you will be the instructor, and since you are totally familiar with your subject, you certainly don't need a scripted Session Plan or even a Combination Plan. You can communicate intelligently about NVC with only occasional reference to some notes. You can't afford not to be organized, however, and you do have a certain design in mind for presenting your topic to your trainees. Therefore, you have decided to use a non-scripted Session Plan. As the project coordinator, then, I'd list your

Figure 21

Procedural Guide to Session Plan Preparation

Session Plan Title	Design Format/Part	Suggested Developer	Assigned To	Date Due
1. _NVC_	1. Non-scripted Introduction	1. User Instructor	1. YOU	1. 6/2
2. _NVC_	2. Non-scripted Procedure	2. User Instructor	2. YOU	2. 6/4
3. _NVC_	3. Non-scripted Practice	3. User Instructor	3. YOU	3. 6/8
4. _NVC_	4. Non-scripted Wrap-Up	4. User Instructor	4. YOU	4. 6/10
5. _____	5. Scripted Introduction	5. User Instructor or Training Writer	5. _____	5. _____
6. _____	6. Scripted Procedure	6. User Instructor or Training Writer	6. _____	6. _____
7. _____	7. Scripted Practice	7. User Instructor or Training Writer	7. _____	7. _____
8. _____	8. Scripted Wrap-Up	8. User Instructor or Training Writer	8. _____	8. _____
9. _____	9. Combination Introduction	9. User Instructor*	9. _____	9. _____
10. _____	10. Combination Procedure	10. User Instructor*	10. _____	10. _____
11. _____	11. Combination Practice	11. User Instructor*	11. _____	11. _____
12. _____	12. Combination Wrap-Up	12. User Instructor*	12. _____	12. _____

session title under the "Session Plan Title" column head at the left of Figure 21. "NVC" appears on lines 1-4 because your entire Session Plan will be non-scripted. If your Session Plan were to be a mixture of all three types, I would simply note the title on the dotted line opposite the appropriate type. As the instructor who will actually be using the NVC Session Plan, and as an expert, you're really the best qualified to write and develop the Session Plan. The "Suggested Developer" is therefore the so-called "User Instructor." To keep my records straight and to conduct periodic follow-ups, I would list your name on dotted lines 1-4 in the "Assigned To" column on the right. Then I would note the dates your assigned session plan parts are due in the far right-hand column under "Date Due."

If I followed this procedure for every Session Plan assigned to every instructor in the course, I could effectively coordinate Session Plan development.

There are additional points to remember about implementing the procedural guide and worksheet. First, Figure 21 illustrates the recommended sequence for developing the four essential parts of a Session Plan. The best sequence is to begin with the introduction and to follow with the procedure, practice, and wrap-up, in that order. This is a logical sequence because it reflects the order in which the Session Plan is eventually used. The sequence is not written in stone, however; if, as the developer, you feel more comfortable writing your Session Plan in a different sequence, then proceed accordingly.

As a general rule, instructors who will actually be using non-scripted Session Plans, as in the above example, are in the best position to write their own. The only exception is when the Session Plan writer ("Training Writer" in Figure 21) is intimately familiar with the instructor's teaching and presentation style. In this situation, the Training Writer can probably prepare an effective non-scripted Session Plan to be used by another instructor.

User Instructors and Training Writers can do an equally effective job of preparing scripted Session Plans. Here the emphasis is on the written word as opposed to the extemporaneous word; on planning rather than on *ad libbing;* on detail rather than on concept. By design, the user instructor either reads or closely references his or her Session Plan.

In most situations, the user instructor can effectively prepare a combination Session Plan. Occasionally, however, the instructor may find it useful to consult a training writer or even to delegate total Session Plan development to a training writer. A user instructor and training writer can even team develop a Session Plan. Since preparing combination Session Plans involves a key decision about the developer, "User Instructor" is highlighted by an asterisk in Figure 21.

User instructors almost always write their own non-scripted Session Plans. User instructors or training writers write their own or another trainer's scripted Session Plans; deciding who the developer should be really isn't too critical. But developers of combination Session Plans should be selected with some thought about whether the user instructor or the training writer will do a better job.

To recap briefly, using scripted, non-scripted, and combination Session Plans in one course or in an entire curriculum has advantages for students, for teachers, and for schools and companies. Preparing Session Plans with the pointers contained in the Developmental Guide section of this book also has many benefits.

VI.

RESOURCES

IN USE AT

Many of the training programs and materials developed by the author and his staff for in-house use feature the kinds of Session Plans described on the previous pages. Additional information about Session Plans may be obtained by contacting Robert G. Godfrey at Allstate Plaza (B6), Northbrook, Illinois 60062.

BOOKS

This volume fills a void that exists because there are so few specific resources available on Session Plans. However, the following related texts will be useful background for teachers and trainers who plan to apply the concepts explained in *Session Plans*. It is recommended that educators who have relatively little experience in incorporating Session Plans in their instructional strategy consult the following resources before actually preparing Session Plans.

1. *The Development and Supervision of Training Programs*
   Homer C. Rose
   Part Two, Chapter 9, "Preparing Courses of Study and Lesson Plans"
   American Technical Society
   1961, 1964

2. *Training by Objectives*
   George S. Odiorne
   Chapter 9, "The Goals-Oriented Lesson Plan"
   The Macmillan Company
   1970

3. *Training and Development Handbook*, Second Edition
   Edited by Robert L. Craig
   Chapter 32, "Job Instruction," by Bird McCord
   McGraw-Hill Book Company
   1976

VII.

APPENDIX
SAMPLE SESSION PLANS

Example of Actual
Non-Scripted Session Plan

"Instruction Techniques" Session Plan

A. Introduction (Lecture) (5 min.)

B. How to select methods and techniques (Lecture and slides) (10 min.)

C. Types of methods and techniques (Lecture and slides) (10 min.)

D. Preparation for videotape presentations (Class) (Time is optional)

E. Videotape presentations (Class (2-3 min. each)

F. Videotape replays (Class) (5 min. each)

    1. Distribute "Trainer Evaluation Checklist."
    2. Have class evaluate each individual's presentation.
    3. Stress the importance of effective evaluation of other trainers.

G. Open discussion regarding lecture and/or presentations (Time is optional)

Example of Actual
Scripted Session Plan

TELEPHONE TECHNIQUES WORKSHOP

```
┌──────────────────────────────────────┐
│  ADMINISTER QUIZ                       │
└──────────────────────────────────────┘

┌──────────────────────────────────────┐
│  REVIEW ANSWERS TO QUIZ                │
└──────────────────────────────────────┘
```

INTRODUCTION TO PART A

Slide 1

Have you ever considered that the telephone is one of your most essential business tools -- a business tool, like the typewriter, that is indispensable? Also, a tool that can either be efficiently and effectively used...or abused? Your business telephone is your basic communications tool. Its proper use enables fast communications, direct communications, and personal communications.

Slide 2

Fast communications in the case of the telephone means instantaneous communications. A memo or letter takes time to deliver, and after being read, additional time is used before a response is received. But through the telephone a reply can be given instantly.

Slide 3

Direct communications implies that there are no chances for deviations of a message, but rather, a message can go from sender to receiver without any other intervening parties who might modify or distort the message.

Slide 4

And personal communications means that a message sender's personality and attitude is readily demonstrated to a receiver as the message is given. But the important thing to remember is that the telephone, as any other tool, can only function optimally if the operator knows how to use it. Today we're going to review how this tool, the business telephone, can be used... efficiently and effectively.

What is efficient telephone usage? Very briefly, efficient telephone usage entails three things:

Slide 5

1. Knowing what features are available in a telephone system,

2. Knowing how to use these features, and

3. Actually using the features economically.

It will be these points that we will cover today.

FOR EFFECTIVE TELEPHONE USAGE
KNOW HOW TO COMMUNICATE
QUICKLY
DIRECTLY
PERSONALLY (COURTEOUSLY)
DO THESE CONSISTENTLY

And what is effective telephone usage? Simply -

1. Knowing how to communicate quickly via
    the telephone,

Slide 6

2. Knowing how to communicate directly
    via the telephone,

3. Knowing how to communicate personally
    (courteously) via the telephone, and
    finally,

4. Actually using the telephone to quickly,
    directly, and personally (courteously)
    communicate with other people.

Why is efficient and effective telephone use so
important? Four very real reasons exist, and
image is the first of these. Let me show you
why image is so important.

Slide 7

```
┌─────────────────────────────────────────┐
│  PLAY TAPE - IMAGE SEGMENT                │
└─────────────────────────────────────────┘

┌─────────────────────────────────────────┐
│  GENERATE COMMENTS IN A GROUP DISCUSSION  │
└─────────────────────────────────────────┘
```

Your efficient and effective use of the telephone
enables you to create a positive image...of your
company and...of yourself. Doesn't it make sense
to always try to reflect only a positive image?

Slide 8

Your efficient and effective use of the phone
also can save time for you and the person you're
communicating with. Remember, two of the phone's
basic features are fast and direct communications.

Slide 9

Furthermore, time does mean money. Our company's
growth and profits are closely tied to this
principle, and through inefficient and ineffective
telephone usage, the costs can be extremely high.

```
WRITE ON CHALKBOARD AND DISCUSS
LOCAL COST INFORMATION SUCH AS:

1.  ANNUAL PHONE BILL

2.  MONTHLY PHONE BILL PER STATION
```

Finally, efficient and effective phone usage offers
you convenience. By using your business phones
properly, telephone communications can become the
easiest method of communication available to you...
surely easier than walking...

Slide 10

...and even easier than writing.

Slide 11

The phone can also be the most accurate method of communication. When you use the phone, misunderstandings can be cleared up instantly.

Slide 12

Although we're meeting today to review one method of business communication -- the telephone -- this should by no means imply that our other business communication methods are unimportant. Depending on the need, letters, memos, and telegrams should also be used efficiently and effectively. Remember, telephone costs can be quite high, while other communication methods might be less costly.

```
GENERATE A GROUP DISCUSSION ABOUT
DISCRETIONARY USE OF ALTERNATIVE
METHODS OF BUSINESS COMMUNICATIONS
```

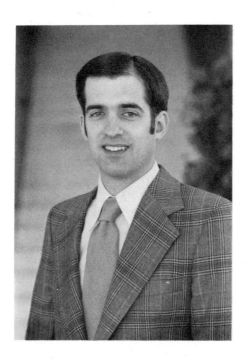

ROBERT G. GODFREY is a Training Project Supervisor with the All-state Insurance Company in Northbrook, Illinois. Mr. Godfrey directs a staff of Training Program Developers who specialize in designing and developing educational and informational programs. Most recently, Mr. Godfrey helped to coordinate the creation and implementation of a five-phase orientation, supervisory, and technical training program for first-line supervisors. In addition, he and his staff have successfully designed and conducted Train the Trainer Workshops, which prepare newly-appointed instructors to become effective trainers. Prior to joining All-State in 1966, Mr. Godfrey was a language arts and social studies teacher in Evanston, Illinois.